A Guide for Using

The Odyssey

in the Classroom

Based on the Classic Epic Poem by Homer

*This guide written by **Stacy Mantle***

Teacher Created Resources, Inc.
6421 Industry Way
Westminster, CA 92683
www.teachercreated.com
ISBN: 978-1-57690-633-0
©*2000 Teacher Created Resources, Inc.*
Reprinted, 2013
Made in U.S.A.

Edited by
Jeri Wilcox
Illustrated by
Howard Chaney
Cover Art by
Charles Adler

The classroom teacher may reproduce copies of the materials in this book for use in a single classroom only. The reproduction of any part of the book for other classrooms or for an entire school or school system is strictly prohibited. No part of this publication may be transmitted, stored, or recorded in any form without written permission from the publisher.

Table of Contents

Introduction 3

Sample Lesson Plans 4

Before the Book (Pre-reading Activities) 5

About the Author 6

Book Summary 7

Vocabulary Lists 8

Vocabulary Activity Ideas 9

Section I (Pre-reading)
- Hands-on Project: Build the Trojan Horse 10
- About the Epic 13
- Curriculum Connections: Literary Techniques in *The Odyssey* 14
- Into Your Life: Characteristics of Epics in Today's Society 15
- Cooperative Learning Activity: Understanding the Epic Hero 16
- Quiz: What Do You Know? 18

Section II (Books I through VI)
- Hands on Project: The Books of *The Odyssey* 19
- Cooperative Learning Activity: Keeping Track of Your Reading 20
- Curriculum Connections: Illustrate *The Odyssey* 21
- Into Your Life: If You Were Odysseus 22
- Quiz: What Do You Know? 23

Section III Books VII through XII)
- Curriculum Connections: Understanding Roman Numerals 24
- Into Your Life: Making Difficult Decisions 25
- Cooperative Learning Activity: The Greeks Had a Word for It 26
- Hands-on Project: Create Your Own Epic 28
- Quiz: What Do You Know? 29

Section IV (Books XIII through XVIII)
- Curriculum Connections: *The Odyssey* in Art 30
- Into Your Life: Fate or Logic 31
- Hands-on Project: The Greek Theater 32
- Cooperative Learning Activity: The Greek Alphabet 33
- Quiz: What Do You Know? 34

Section V (Books XIX through XXIV)
- Curriculum Connections: Great Greek Food 35
- Cooperative Learning Activity: Map the Journey 36
- Hands-on Project: Create a Travel Brochure 38
- Into Your Life: What Would You Do? 39
- Quiz: What Do You Know? 40

Suggest Research Topics 41

Culminating Activities 42

Unit Test Options 43

Bibliography and Resources 46

Answer Key 47

Introduction

The Odyssey has everything that an avid reader could wish for: lively characters, wise heroes, the entire world as its setting, and even cantankerous gods. It is a story of perseverance and endurance and teaches not only good literature, but also a respect for life and the courage to continue on in the face of adversity.

There are many excellent versions of *The Odyssey* that you can obtain from the library or bookstore. The version that was used in preparing this module is the translation by Robert Fagles, which is published by Penguin Publications. Other versions can be downloaded free of charge from the Internet from a number of different sites. Refer to the bibliography for Web site listings.

In Literature Units, great care has been taken to select pieces of literature which the reader can come to appreciate and enjoy.

Teachers who use this unit will find the following features to supplement their own valuable ideas:

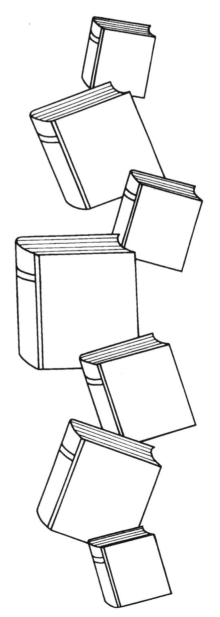

- Sample Lesson Plans

- Pre-reading Activities

- Biographical Sketch of the Author

- Book Summary

- Vocabulary Lists and Activities

- Chapters grouped for study with activities including the following:

    —a quiz
    —a hands-on project
    —a cooperative learning activity
    —a cross-curricular connection
    —an extension into the reader's life

- Post reading activities

- Research Ideas

- Culminating Activity

- Three Unit Test Options

- Bibliography and Resource section

- Answer Key

We are certain that this unit will be a worthwhile addition to your planning, and we hope that as you use our ideas, your students will increase their appreciation of good literature.

Sample Lesson Plans

The following lessons are suggestions only. *The Odyssey* is a lengthy poem and can take months, even years, to fully understand. We have found that in teaching *The Odyssey*, it is best to assign the reading of certain sections, while discussing and reviewing the more difficult books as a class. This, of course, will vary according to the length of time available to teach *The Odyssey* and the level of students that you are working with. Examples of reading sections are listed below, and they can be used in conjunction with the Hallmark movie presentation of *The Odyssey*, which can be rented at your local video store.

Week 1

❑ Discuss the background of the epic. (page 13)

❑ Read and discuss "About the Author." (page 6)

❑ Discuss the history of *The Odyssey*. (page 7)

❑ Introduce the first week's vocabulary. (page 8)

❑ Discuss the reading "In Media Res." (page 10)

❑ Complete "Build the Trojan Horse" activity. (page 11)

❑ Complete "Characteristics of Epics in Today's Society." (page 15)

Week 2

❑ Assign reading (books I–VI)

❑ Introduce vocabulary for Section II. (page 8)

❑ Discuss the characteristics of an epic hero. (pages 16 and 17)

❑ Discuss notes on reading. (page 20)

Week 3

❑ Assign reading of books VII–XII

❑ Introduce vocabulary for Section III. (page 8)

❑ Complete worksheet, "The Greeks Had a Word for It." (page 26)

❑ Have students complete their own epic. (page 28)

Week 4

❑ Assign reading of books XIII–XVIII

❑ Introduce vocabulary for Section IV. (page 8)

❑ Discuss notes on reading. (page 18)

❑ Complete hands-on-project, "The Greek Theater." (page 32)

Week 5

❑ Assign reading of books XIX–XXIV.

❑ Introduce vocabulary for Section V. (page 8)

❑ Complete map activity. (page 36)

❑ Complete travel brochure. (page 38)

Week 6

❑ Complete Research Project. (page 41)

❑ Complete two of the supplemental activities. (page 42)

❑ Do unit exams. (page 43)

Before the Book

The Odyssey is an epic poem and can be somewhat overwhelming even to the most accomplished high school student. It is important to raise the student's excitement level regarding the book. This can be accomplished in several ways, many of which are listed below.

Activities

Watch the movie prior to reading the poem. This raises the levels of excitement and interest for the students, and it prepares them for the complicated text of the poem. An excellent movie version of *The Odyssey* by Hallmark Presentations can be found in your local video stores.

Plan a Greek Festival

Assign each group an activity, food, and game that they are responsible for researching and planning. This can be a great experience for the entire school! There are several methods of planning a Greek festival. Several sources to use for planning are listed in the bibiliography.

Knowledge of Mythology

Prior to reading *The Odyssey,* the students should have a thorough background on the names and characteristics of the Greek and Roman gods. Reviewing a unit on mythology is recommended.

The Epic

The characteristics of an epic poem should be discussed, as well as the logic behind it. You should also discuss the various techniques of poetry. See "About the Epic" on page 13.

Work in Groups

Working in groups can be very beneficial to helping understanding. Assign each group one book to read, then allow them to do a graded presentation on that book. Another method is to assign each group a different book, take notes, and share the results with the other students. This provides the necessary background information, while maximizing class time.

History

A good background on the history of *The Odyssey,* ancient Greece and Rome, and the geography that *The Odyssey* covers is indispensable. You may also need to review the main concepts of mythology and the ancient gods and goddesses of Greece. *The Odyssey* is best studied during a shared unit with history and mythology. Homer's poem is an ideal way of understanding the ways of life and the belief system—as well as the political structure—of Greece. Geography also plays an important part in *The Odyssey* as the reader explores the journey of Odysseus. Collaborate with other teachers in making this unit work.

Language

When reading *The Odyssey*, it is important to remember that many authors have translated it into many different languages over several hundred years. This results in different interpretations of text. Spelling can also vary dramatically. Make sure that your students understand this. A thorough understanding of vocabulary is very necessary to comprehending *The Odyssey*.

About the Author

There are many thoughts on who Homer actually was. Some scholars believe that he was a blind man who lived in Greece around 700 B.C. Others believe that Homer was actually an embodiment of several different men, all of whom collaborated on the two epic poems entitled *The Iliad* and *The Odyssey*. We may never know who Homer truly was. Seven different city-states in Greece each claimed the honor of being Homer's birthplace, but if Homer ever did exist, he probably lived in Chios. The dialect used in *The Odyssey* is that of Asian Ionian Greek, which was common in the area of Chios at the time this epic was written.

Common thought is that *The Iliad* was written approximately 750 B.C. and *The Odyssey* some 30 years later, around 720 B.C. Most likely, the epic poem was composed during this time, and then written out centuries later. If this is true, then Homer wrote about a very different time than the one in which he lived. During 720 B.C., Greece consisted of scattered, independent city-states. This poem appears to chronicle the "Golden Age" of Greece. In *The Odyssey*, Homer describes an aristocratic society. This is first seen on the island of Ithaca, when after Odysseus departs, the society of the island becomes chaotic. Penelope, Odysseus' wife, is alone and frightened, and Telemachus is too young to assume leadership. Combined with the arrival of the suitors, the small society is thrown into turmoil, and only the return of Odysseus or the interference of the gods can return the society to normal.

During the Homeric Age, there were very few people who could read and write, and so stories were passed down orally. This is the reason that nearly all writing was put into the form of poetry. Rhyme is easier to remember. Sometimes these stories were read in the form of plays. These plays were performed in a Greek theater, and the actors wore masks and high platform shoes, which forced them to move around very slowly. The theater had no scenery, was out in the open air, and had no actresses—only actors. There were only two types of plays: tragedies and comedies. One of the favorite tragedies was about the Trojan War, which is the first topic that Homer wrote about. The challenge presented to poets was to tell an old story in a new and exciting way, which Homer does most effectively.

We have, over the last 3,000 years, only possessed about 6 to 10 great epics. Two of these are by Homer. Aristotle once said that the epic ranked second only to tragedy, and many people still agree.

The Odyssey

The Odyssey was probably written in the 700s B.C. and was originally an oral work. It was translated from Greek in the 1500s. Beginning in the 6th Century B.C., *The Odyssey* was recited annually in a Greek festival. It was also recited in a number of different readings to royalty throughout the year, each poet telling it in a slightly different way. This accounts for the various translations of *The Odyssey*.

The Odyssey begins with an invocation to the muses (goddesses of inspiration for literature and art). "Sing in me, O Muses, and through me tell the story of that man skilled in all ways of contending. . ."

This is the story of Odysseus, wise and noble King of Ithaca, who reluctantly sails with his army to take part in the rescue of Helen after she is kidnapped by Prince Paris.

In his abrupt departure, Odysseus leaves behind a pregnant wife, Penelope, with instructions that if he should not return, she should remarry, so that his newborn son may be brought up properly. She reluctantly agrees.

After ten years of bloody war, the Achean heroes are finally free to sail for home. When *The Odyssey* begins, an additional decade has passed since the other chieftains of Odysseus' army have returned, without their leader. In the absence of Odysseus, noblemen from throughout the world learn of Penelope's lost husband, and flock to the city of Ithaca to win her hand. The suitors are a greedy lot, and they are interested mainly in the wealth and the power that goes along with her station in life.

She, ever faithful to Odysseus, finds many beguiling ways to avoid the hands of these suitors as they remain at her palace, determined to stay until she chooses one of them for her husband. They waste the resources of her palace, eating her food, drinking her wine, and taking liberties with the women at the palace. She is powerless to evict them, but Telemachus, the son of Odysseus and Penelope, has grown while his father is away, and he is determined to locate his father.

Meanwhile, during these ten lost years, Odysseus has wandered throughout the world, forbidden to return home by Poseidon, Lord of the Seas. He survives a number of events and disasters by using his wit and intelligence. However, all of his ships and men have been lost. This story details his journey through the oceans of this world, until finally, with the aid of the King of the Phaecians, Odysseus is able to return to Ithaca. Assisted by Athena, Odysseus is able to punish the  suitors, and reestablish himself as King of Ithaca. Reunited with his wife and son, and with the intervention of the gods and goddesses, Odysseus is able to thwart a civil war while reclaiming his place as the king.

Vocabulary Lists

These are examples of vocabulary words that you may wish to introduce. Although these words are common in many versions of *The Odyssey*, they may not be found in all of them. Review your version of *The Odyssey* before assigning them to students.

Book I–VI

tempest	rash	mentor
herald	portal	lotus
nectar	portent	muses
laurel	machinations	abate
lamented	preeminent	distaff
libation	tribulation	
asunder	prudent	

Books VII–XII

retribution	abominable
suppliant	perdition
cuckold	precipitous
affliction	injunction
gaffer	minx
conspicuous	ambrosia
eloquence	nymph
winnowing	cuckold
mess	cudgel

Books XIII–XVIII

fettle	lacrimation
humiliate	consecrated
interminable	illustrious
reproach	requite
ravenous	indefatigable
presumption	insatiable

Books XIX–XXIV

chafes	doughty
grimace	execration
unabashed	perplexity
propriety	contemptuous
manifestly	

8

Vocabulary Activity Ideas

Acting Out: Have one group of students act out each word, as other students attempt to guess the word.

Find a Passage: Have students locate a passage that exemplifies or illustrates each word. This passage should be written, and students should explain why they selected that passage.

Writing it out: The students complete a paragraph describing a day in their lives using five of the listed words. This exercise can be used for each of the vocabulary sections.

Synonyms/Antonyms: The students find at least one synonym and one antonym for each word. This should be listed in spreadsheet form. This activity also teaches the use of a thesaurus. An example is listed below.

Vocabulary	Synonym	Antonym
temptation	entice	repel
ravenous	hungry	full
mentor	teacher	student

Vocabulary Journal: Have the students maintain a vocabulary journal. Each time they run across a word that is unfamiliar to them, they should write it out and locate the definition as it applies to the story.

Illustrate the word: Have students "visualize" what the word sounds like, and then draw a picture of what they see.

Assign a word: Have students assign a word to each character. This word should symbolize the character, and would be similar to an epithet. (For example, Penelope = lament.)

Games: Have each student design a word search or crossword puzzle using each of their vocabulary words.

Jeopardy: This is always a fun game for students. Have one team write answers, while the other teams come up with questions.

Parts of Speech Chart: Students will create a graph with the vocabulary words listed under the proper headings of noun, adjective, verb, etc.

Build the Trojan Horse

In Media Res

The Odyssey begins "in media res," or "in the middle of things," and therefore, in order to understand *The Odyssey*, it is necessary to have a basic understanding of *The Iliad*. *The Iliad* was another epic poem about the Trojan War that Homer composed prior to writing *The Odyssey*. Many events that occur in *The Odyssey* are a direct result of events that happened during the Trojan War. The following is a very short synopsis of the Trojan War, and the events that influenced the second epic poem from Homer, *The Odyssey*.

Prince Paris was a young man who faced a challenge. He was asked to judge who the most beautiful woman in the world was, and he was given three women from whom to choose: Aphrodite, the goddess of love; Hera, wife of Zeus; and Athena, goddess of wisdom and war.

Each woman offered Prince Paris a bribe if he would choose her, but Aphrodite offered him the greatest prize: Helen of Troy, the most beautiful mortal woman in the world. So Prince Paris selected Aphrodite as the winner and claimed his prize by abducting Helen of Troy. The problem was that Helen of Troy was already married to King Menelaus. King Menelaus, determined to reclaim his wife, gathered his army and went after Prince Paris and Helen. These are the events that began the Trojan War.

Odysseus did not want to join in the battle but was finally persuaded. Reluctantly, he left his wife and newborn son to sail to Troy and fight in the Trojan War.

After ten years of war, Odysseus decided that they would tear down their ships to build a great wooden horse. The Trojans would then believe they had left and would accept the horse as a gift. Just as Odysseus predicted, the Trojans believed that the Greeks were offering them a gift and admitting defeat. So, they took the huge wooden horse into the city gates. When the city of Troy fell asleep after a long night of celebrating their victory, Greek warriors climbed out of the huge wooden horse and attacked them.

This incident symbolizes Odysseus's intellect and ability to command. Odysseus is not only strong of body, he is strong of mind, and this is what makes him a valuable person. Odysseus commanded his men justly and fairly, and most importantly wisely. He is admired for this quality, and this is why his men are willing to follow him even to the depths of Hades in the epic journey of *The Odyssey*.

Build the Trojan Horse *(cont.)*

Odysseus created the monster Trojan horse in order to hide from his enemies and catch them by surprise. He and his crew ripped apart their ships, then spent many days building the huge wooden horse. They climbed into the belly of the wooden animal and waited until the Trojans wheeled them into the city of Troy. After a long night of drinking and eating, the Trojans passed out on the dirt floors. The Greeks, led by Odysseus, then climbed out of the wooden horse and killed all of the people in their sleep. This is the event that ends *The Iliad*, and it leads us to the beginning of *The Odyssey*.

Now is your chance to create a model of the Trojan horse that Odysseus built from his ship. You will need the following materials:

- butcher paper
- pencils
- rulers

1. Decide on the size of the horse that you would like to build. You will need to decide on a measurement that represents the larger size. For instance, 1" = 1'. In this way, you will be able to build your horse to scale.

2. Create a layout on a piece of paper, depicting what the finished product will look like. You will draw out the basic design (not to scale) so that you have a model to follow.

3. Complete measurements of the legs, body, and head. Remember that the base of the horse will need to be sturdy enough to hold the men who will be inside, and will also need to support the entire structure. Research what size you will need your finished horse to be. A math teacher or shop teacher can help you in this area.

4. A good plan is to place wheels on the bottom of the horse or to build it on a sled of some kind. The Trojans will need to be able to move the large beast into the city.

5. Remember to include a way into and out of the body of the horse. The men need to be able to access it.

6. Now you may begin your actual "plan." Check all of your measurements, and make sure that your picture includes each measurement. An example follows on the next page.

7. Remember that this is a group project. Cooperate with your fellow students on the design of your Trojan horse.

8. When the horse design is complete, display it with pride! You may wish to build the actual horse using the plans that you have created.

The Trojan Horse Design Plan

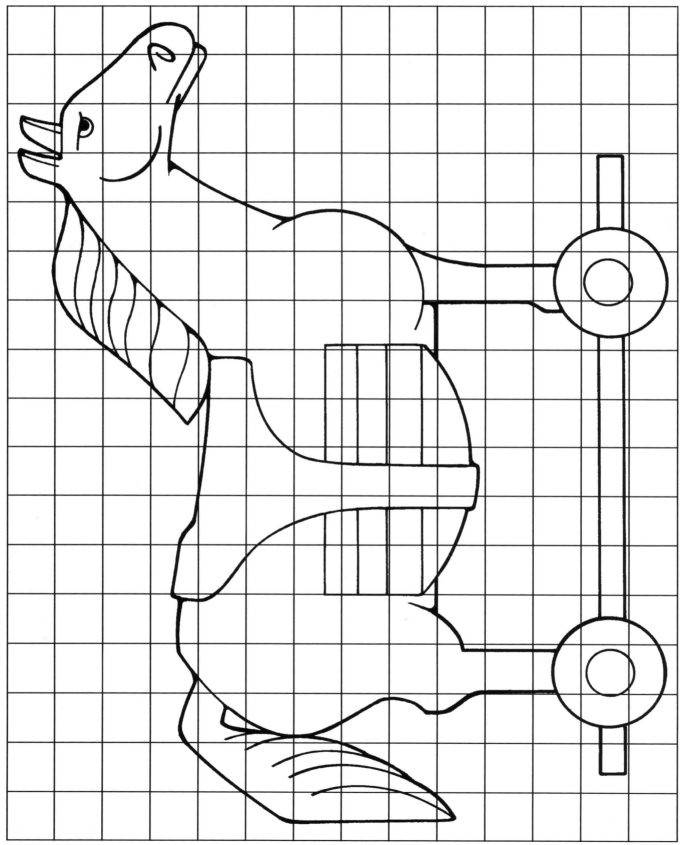

About the Epic

An epic is a long, narrative poem, which contains the following characteristics:

1. *It contains adventure.*

2. *It has a central heroic figure.*

3. *The setting is vast—often covering the entire world.*
   (*The Odyssey* even includes a journey to Hades.)

4. *Supernatural forces (gods) are involved.*

5. *An elevated style is used (a serious tone of voice).*

And so, it is essentially a long, narrative poem that covers a vast amount of territory over an extended period of time. Scholars later divided Homer's work into 24 "books," and that has become the standard for any epic poem written. The epic has a standard measure of verse and is written in dactylic hexameter. This means that it has five metrical feet in each line. The first five feet may consist of either a dactyl (a heavy syllable followed by two light ones, - - -), or a spondee (two long sounds, – –). Regardless of the pattern used, each line must end in a spondee. This results in each line having between twelve to seventeen syllables, depending on the number of dactyls and spondees used.

The Odyssey is filled with literary techniques that are now the standard for all epic poetry. These include:

Epithets: A repeated description oftentimes was used to meet rhyming/meter requirements (e.g., "rosy-fingered dawn," "wise Odysseus," and "bright-eyed Athena"). Poets devised this method to fulfill the metrical requirements of a poem without changing the meaning of a line. They were also very easy to remember for actors who recited the poetry.

Similes: A comparison of a subject, to something more easily visualized or more familiar to the audience. A simile is easy to recognize, as it always uses the words "like" or "as" (e.g., "Then he advanced on them like a mountain lion who sallies out, defying wind and rain in the pride of his power . . . ").

Formal Rhetoric: Long, formal speeches by the characters. (This technique is often used in public speeches.) These can be found throughout *The Odyssey* and are used to better establish the character who speaks. Long speeches are also more practical than short spurts of dialogue between characters and are much easier to memorize and recite.

Literary Techniques in
The Odyssey

The Odyssey uses many different poetic techniques to accomplish its aim. Several of these are the epithet, the simile, and formal rhetoric. Using what you have learned from page 13, complete the following activity.

Activity: See if you can find 10 examples of epithets, similes, and formal rhetoric during your reading of *The Odyssey*. Use the following graph to record your findings.

Example	Page #	Quote
epithet	31	"bright-eyed Athena"

Characteristics of Epics in Today's Society

Remember that an epic has the following characteristics:

1. *It contains adventure.*
2. *It has a central heroic figure.*
3. *The setting is vast—often covering the entire world.*
4. *Supernatural forces (gods) are involved.*
5. *An elevated style is used (a serious tone of voice).*

Think of a television show or a movie that you have seen, which has all of the characteristics of an epic. One example would be the classic *Moby Dick* based on the novel by Herman Melville.

Moby Dick

1. It contains adventure: A man is forced to confront and destroy his enemy, a terrifying whale, while braving the oceans of the world.
2. It has a central heroic figure: Ahab Captain of the *Pequod*.
3. The setting is vast: It covers most of the world.
4. Supernatural forces are involved: The sea is portrayed as its own character.
5. An elevated style is used: The novel is narrated by Ishmael.

What other books, movies, or television shows can you find that illustrate the characteristics of an epic?

Item and Title: _____

Adventure: _____

Heroic Figure: _____

Setting: _____

Supernatural Forces: _____

Narration: _____

Into Your Life

How is your life like an epic?_____

_____

Does your life have any of the characteristics of an epic? _____

_____

Which ones? Explain in detail how your life fits the characteristics of an epic. _____

_____

Understanding the Epic Hero

A true epic hero uses only two things: the tools at his immediate disposal, and his mind. In *The Odyssey*, Odysseus embodies the Greek ideas of a "strong mind in a strong body." He is someone who nobly represents a balance of physical and intellectual possibilities, or what a man can and should be.

As you read, complete the following chart about the characteristics of Odysseus.

Characteristics of Odysseus, the Epic Hero		
Adventure	**Evidence of Physical Ability**	**Evidence of Intellectual Prowess**
The Lotus Eaters		
The Cyclops	Working together to put out the eye of the Cyclops with a long staff	Singing to the Cyclops and offering him wine to lull him asleep Offering the name of "Noman" shows foresight
The Sirens		
Scylla		
Charybdis		

Understanding the Epic Hero *(cont.)*

What do you think the qualities of an epic hero are? Make a list below of each quality, and then check off the ones that Odysseus has, and the ones that each person listed has.

List three people that you believe have epic hero qualities, and explain why you chose each.

Qualities	Odysseus	U.S. Presidents	Yourself	Your Friend

What Do You Know?

After reading each question decide if the answer is **true** or **false**. Circle the correct answer.

1. **True** or **False:** The epic is a long, narrative poem covering a vast amount of territory.

2. **True** or **False:** In an epic, a nation's fate to some degree depends upon the actions of a hero.

3. **True** or **False:** Aristotle ranked the epic as second only to comedy.

4. **True** or **False:** Despite numerous attempts over 3,000 years, we possess only a half dozen or so epics of greatness.

5. **True** or **False:** The settings of epics are never larger than the world.

6. **True** or **False:** The heroes in epics always use weapons to accomplish great feats.

7. **True** or **False:** In an epic, the poet often begins by stating an invocation to the gods for help.

8. **True** or **False:** "In media res" means "beginning in the middle of things."

9. **True** or **False:** The Trojan War occurred after *The Odyssey* begins.

10. **True** or **False:** Epics never contain similes.

11. **True** or **False:** Heroic poem is another name for epic.

12. **True** or **False:** The entire text of *The Odyssey* is written in verse (poetry form).

The Books of *The Odyssey*

The Odyssey is divided into 24 sections, or books. As they are lengthy, and sometimes complex, it will be helpful to keep a short list of notes on each one. The next two pages are designed to help you keep track of your reading.

Assign each book a title as you complete the reading. For example, Book IV might be called "The Red-Haired King and His Lady."

Book #	Title
I	
II	
III	
IV	
V	
VI	
VII	
VIII	
IX	
X	
XI	
XII	
XIII	
XIV	
XV	
XVI	
XVII	
XVIII	
XIX	
XX	
XXI	
XXII	
XXIII	
XXIV	

Keeping Track of Your Reading

Use this sheet to keep track of your reading during *The Odyssey*.

Book #: _____ Title: _____

Characters: _____

Brief description of characters: _____

_____

Major events that occur in this book: _____

_____

_____

_____

_____

_____

_____

_____

_____

_____

_____

_____

_____

_____

_____

Setting: _____

Notes and Ideas: _____

This sheet can be reproduced for each book of *The Odyssey*.

Illustrate *The Odyssey*

During 700 B.C., there were very few people who could read and write. Many citizens kept records by recording their thoughts in simplistic drawings. Keep track of your reading by illustrating each book of *The Odyssey*. Try to include the setting, the characters, the events, and the gods/goddesses that have a place in this book. Also, include Odysseus and his role during this book. When you have finished, you will have a book of 24 pages of illustrations that you can share with your friends. You may wish to bind your book and make a cover for it.

If You Were Odysseus

Write a short essay on what you would do if you were Odysseus at this point. Would you stay with Calypso and become immortal? Or would you try to return to your family no matter the cost? Use this page to write your essay. When you are finished, explain orally why you feel this way to a classmate who has chosen an opposite answer.

What Do You Know?

1. Whom does Homer ask for help in telling his tale? _____

2. How long has Odysseus been gone? _____

3. Who does Athena disguise herself as in Book I? _____

4. When Telemachus threatens to punish the suitors in Book II, what are the omens that appear?

   _____

5. Whom does Antinous blame for the suitors' bad behavior? _____

6. How does Penelope avoid picking one of the suitors? _____

   _____

7. What does Athena tell Telemachus to do? _____

   _____

8. What do Antinous and Eurymachus plan to do to Telemachus? _____

   _____

9. Which god is most against Odysseus? _____

10. Who is the red-haired king in book IV? _____

11. Who is the goddess who helps Odysseus? _____

12. What does Calypso offer to Odysseus if he will stay with her? _____

13. Where does King Nestor live? _____

14. What does King Nestor offer in sacrifice to Zeus? _____

15. When Telemachus and Peisitratus arrive at the palace of Menelaus, what do they find?

   _____

16. Which god is dispatched to tell Odysseus that he will be allowed to return home? _____

   _____

17. Where does Calypso live? _____

18. Where does Odysseus go after leaving Calypso and after being shipwrecked?_____

   _____

19. Who discovers Odysseus when he washes up in Scheria? _____

   _____

20. Why does Nasicaa decide to wash the marriage linen? _____

   _____

Understanding Roman Numerals

Roman numerals are used to separate each section of *The Odyssey*. We still use Roman numerals today in many different ways. For example, we use Roman numerals for outlines, and many people use them in business. This section will teach you how to count using Roman numerals.

I = 1	L = 50	M = 1000
V = 5	C = 100	
X = 10	D = 500	

The Roman system of counting relies on the above main numbers. Each number is then added or subtracted by placing others in front (for subtracting) or behind (for adding). Examples are shown below:

III = 1 + 1 + 1 = 3

IV = 5 − 1 = 4

CV = 100 + 5 = 105

LX = 50 + 10 = 60

MD = 1000 + 500 = 1500

The order of operations is defined by the fact that there are no negative numbers in this type of math. This is how you know whether to add or subtract. If you come up with a negative number, you should have done the opposite function.

What if you have more than two or three numbers? Okay, at this point it gets a little more complicated.

Let's say you have this number: **MCDXCII**. Remember, always read from left to right, and if a smaller number is to the *immediate* left of a larger number, then subtract that smaller number from the larger number.

Step 1: M = **1000**

Step 2: C = 100 and D = 500; and so CD = 500 − 100, or **400**
   Result: **MCD = 1400**

Step 3: X = 10 and C =100; and so XC = 100 − 10, or **90**
   Result: **MCDXC = 1490**

Step 4: II = 2
   Result: **MCDXCII = 1492**

Now you can find the numbers for other things. Try the exercise below to test your knowledge of Roman numerals.

1. 15 ____		5. 280 ____		9. 48 ____	
2. 759 ____		6. 493 ____		10. 390 ____	
3. 2000 ____		7. 2050 ____		11. 224 ____	
4. 1029 ____		8. 928 ____		12. 749 ____	

Making Difficult Decisions

Odysseus is forced to make many difficult decisions. Sometimes, he is tempted to choose the easy way, but he almost always comes to his senses and stays on the right path. For example, when Odysseus is offered immortality by the beautiful nymph Calypso, he chooses instead to return to his waiting wife. When he departs the island, his small boat is overturned and he somehow manages to swim for two days before finally coming to rest on the beach of Princess Nausicaa. But, he never gives up his quest to return home. How would you handle the following situations?

Find a solution to the following problems:

1. You are trapped by a person in your school who is a fighter. You don't want to fight, and besides, the bully is much bigger than you are. How do you remove yourself from this situation without hurting yourself or others? _____

   _____

   _____

   _____

   _____

2. Your boyfriend/girlfriend has gone to fight in a war and has disappeared for twenty long years. You promised him/her that you would find someone else if he/she didn't return, but your heart still belongs to him/her. Do you fulfill your promise by waiting for your loved one's return, or do you find another? _____

   _____

   _____

   _____

   _____

3. Every time you try to do what is right, it appears that something stands in your way. Do you continue to do your best, or do you give up? _____

   _____

   _____

   _____

   _____

4. Your father, whom you have never seen, has been away for 20 years. Your mother is very upset, and your house is torn upside down by men who want to marry her. What do you do: Search for a father you have never met, or resign yourself to your fate? _____

   _____

   _____

   _____

   _____

The Greeks Had a Word For It

The English language has been enriched by many contributions from the Greek language. The sciences, geography, and the theater have all prospered as we have drawn from other languages. Complete the following worksheet to find some of the connections!

1. Write the meanings of these common Greek prefixes.

mono- _____   photo- _____

kilo- _____   bio- _____

poly- _____   chrono- _____

bi - _____   octa- _____

hemi- _____   auto- _____

neo- _____   tele- _____

tri - _____   homo- _____

phil- _____   syn- _____

penta- _____   deca- _____

psycho _____   mega- _____

hexa- _____   micro- _____

2. Write the meanings of these common Greek suffixes:

-graph _____   -sphere _____

-gram _____   -phone _____

-onym _____   -gon _____

-scope _____   -meter _____

-logy _____

The Greeks Had a Word For It *(cont.)*

3. Now you can be a word-maker. If you know the Greek roots and prefixes, you can easily discover the meanings of many words. Study these examples.

astrology = astro (star) + logy (study of) = study of the stars.

polygon = poly (many) + gon (sided) = many sided.

Use what you know about Greek roots and prefixes to work out the meanings of these words.

autograph _____

homonym _____

biology _____

hemisphere _____

pentagon _____

psychology _____

polyphonic _____

autobiography _____

photomete _____

neophyte _____

telescope _____

chronological _____

kilometer _____

Find ten other words, which are made up of Greek parts. Write them and their meanings on the lines below.

1. _____

2. _____

3. _____

4. _____

5. _____

6. _____

7. _____

9. _____

10. _____

Create Your Own Epic

Everyone's life is similar to an epic. We all begin a very long journey, which is filled with adventure and spans a great length of time. With these characteristics in mind, write a short essay on how your life is an epic. Although you may not have lived for a long time, you have already had many adventures. Include how you believe your life will continue on this epic journey. Will you become a successful business person; explore a newly discovered abyss at the bottom of the sea or maybe become a doctor, saving the lives of others?

You may want to begin your essay with one of the following sentences:

> My life is like an epic because . . .
>
> My epic adventure began on the day I was born . . .
>
> Everyone engages on a journey of life. My life journey began in the town of . . .

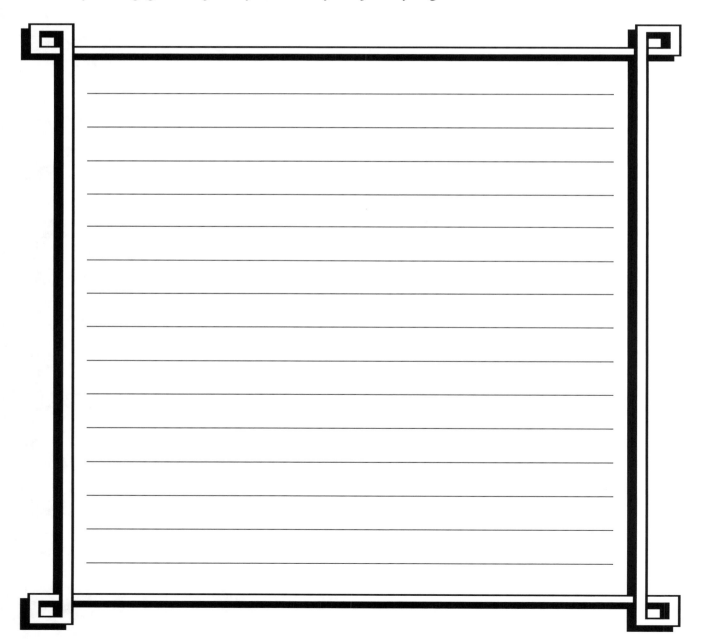

What Do You Know?

1. What happened to men who ate of the Lotus? _____

_____

2. Why does Odysseus call himself "Noman"?_____

_____

3. What is the Cyclops's name?_____

4. Who is the father of the Cyclops? _____

5. Who is Aeolus? _____

_____

6. Where was Odysseus when cannibals attacked him? _____

7. Where does Circe live? _____

8. What did Circe turn Odysseus's men into? _____

_____

9. Whom did Odysseus seek in Hades? _____

10. What are the Sirens? _____

_____

11. Describe how the men face and overcome the song of the Sirens. _____

_____

12. What is Charybdis? _____

13. What is Scylla? _____

14. What is Helios's threat to the gods? _____

_____

15. Where did Telemachus go to find out about his father? _____

_____

16. Who helps Odysseus and gives him advice?_____

17. What does Odysseus do when he introduces himself to his son? _____

_____

18. How does Telemachus react when Odysseus returns home? _____

_____

The Odyssey in Art

Books VII–XII chronicle an exciting time in Odysseus' life. He meets a number of new creatures such as the Polyphemos (the Cyclops), Circes (the witch), Scylla (the six-headed monster), and Charybdis (the whirlpool); and he even explores the underworld of Hades. Choose four of the following scenes to draw a detailed picture of the place as described by Homer. The picture must look just as Homer describes it in his poem.

1. the cave of Scylla, the six-headed monster
2. the island of the Cattle of the Sun God
3. the underworld of Hades
4. the Island of the Lotus Eaters
5. the Palace of Circes, the witch

6. the cave of Polyphemus, the Cyclops
7. the palace of Odysseus and Penelope
8. the boat of Odysseus
9. the whirlpool, Charybdis
10. the island of Ithaca

Fate or Logic?

There are many obstacles in the path of Odysseus during his journey. Some people would say that fate is against him, and no matter what Odysseus does, he has no control over the ultimate outcome. Other people see that Odysseus remains determined to overcome everything that is dealt to him and therefore creates his own fate. What type of a person are you? Do you take responsibility for your life, or do you resign yourself to fates? Think about how you would handle each of the following situations, and then write down your answers.

Situation 1: You have arrived late to school (again) because your mom didn't wake you up in time to catch the bus (again). You end up getting detention because you were late, and now you are stuck staying after school while your friends have gone to the new mall. Answer the following questions:

1. Is it fate or your own actions that made you late for school? _____

_____

2. Is it fate or your own actions that caused you to receive detention? _____

_____

3. Will you attend detention? _____

_____

4. What will you do while you are there? _____

_____

5. Read over your answers and decide if they show that you create your own fate or react to situations as they occur. _____

Situation 2: Your best friend has just told you that a gang is harassing him on the way home from school.

1. Is it fate or your friend's own actions that cause him to be harassed? _____

_____

2. How will you advise your friend to correct the situation? _____

_____

3. How will you take part in helping your friend out? _____

_____

Situation 3: Your best friend has just told you that she is drinking heavily on the weekends. You know that she comes from a bad home and her parents are not exactly reliable.

1. Is it fate or your friend's own actions that caused her to start drinking? _____

_____

2. How will you advise your friend to correct the situation? _____

_____

3. How will you take part in helping your friend out? _____

_____

The Greek Theater

During the age of Homer, the theater came into existence. Generally, plays were dedicated to the great Dionysus (god of wine), and an annual contest for the best tragedy was established.

Poetry readings became increasingly popular during this time as well, and Homer's *The Iliad* was a favorite. But what if *The Odyssey* had been written in another form? What if the famous epic poem had originally been a play or a song? Choose one of the following activities. Work in groups of 4–5 people and choose one project. Other classmates will evaluate each group using the rubric at the bottom of the page.

1. Compose the theme of *The Odyssey* into the lyrics of an existing song. Include the main events of the epic poem as well as each element of the epic. Be creative, and use a format with which you are familiar. Choose from rap, classical, country, or any other type of music you enjoy.

2. Re-enact one scene from your favorite book of *The Odysssey*. Create a written script and, along with the members of your group, act it out. Develop costumes, if necessary.

Try not to read from your script during your performance. Remember, great performers were able to recite the entire text of *The Odyssey* by memory, in Greek, during one very long evening.

Rubric for Evaluating	
5. Excellent	Includes the main concepts of the poem, explores at least three events that occurred during *The Odyssey*, is interesting to watch, and contains visual aids. The reader rarely refers to his/her notes. Demonstrates a great amount of creativity. Obviously a great deal of thought went into this presentation.
4. Very good	Includes the main concepts of the poem, explores at least two events that occurred during *The Odyssey*, and is fun to watch. The reader occasionally refers to his/her notes during the performance. Demonstrates creativity.
3. Good	Includes the main concepts of the poem, and explores at least one event that occurred during *The Odyssey*. The performer reads from a prepared script, but is able to maintain our attention.
2. Fair	Includes the main concepts of *The Odyssey*, and explores at least one event. Needs more thought placed into the presentation.
1. Needs improvement	The theme of *The Odyssey* and its events are not explored or presented. No visual aids are used. Very little time was spent in preparation for this assignment.

The Greek Alphabet

We can attribute nearly 12% of the English language to Greek roots. Some examples include alphabet, barbarian, history, chronology, and drama. The Greek alphabet was taken from Phoenician script during the eighth century BC. Here is the Greek alphabet in its entirety.

The Greek Alphabet

Lowercase	Capital	Name	Modern
α	A	alpha	a
β	B	beta	b
γ	Γ	gamma	c, g
δ	Δ	delta	d
ε	E	epsilon	e
ζ	Z	zeta	z
η	H	eta	h, e
θ	Θ	theta	th
ι	I	iota	j, i
κ	K	kappa	k
λ	Λ	lambda	l
μ	M	mu	m
ν	N	nu	n
ξ	Ξ	xi	x
o	O	omicron	o
π	Π	pi	p
ρ	P	rho	r
σ	Σ	sigma	s
τ	T	tau	t
υ	Y	upsilon	u, v, w, y
φ	Φ	phi	f, ph, q
χ	X	chi	ch
ψ	Ψ	psi	ps
ω	Ω	omega	o

See what the following words would look like using Greek letters:

The Odyssey _____

Your name_____

Your school name _____

Write a letter to a friend or classmate about *The Odyssey*, but attempt to write it using only Greek letters.

What Do You Know?

1. How is Odysseus finally transported to his home of Ithaca? _____

   _____

2. Who meets Odysseus on the beach of Ithaca? _____

3. How is she disguised? _____

4. What happens to the Phaecians when Poseidon finds out how they helped Odysseus? _____

   _____

5. Who is the first person to whom Odysseus shows his true identity? _____

   _____

6. What happens when Odysseus, in disguise, sees his dog, Argus? _____

   _____

   _____

7. Who is the one person who denies food to Odysseus during the feast in Book XVII? _____

   _____

8. Why does the beggar, Irus, deny Odysseus favors? _____

   _____

   _____

9. What does Homer attempt to represent when he depicts Argus toothless, helpless, and lying in a

   pile of filth? _____

   _____

   _____

10. How does the nurse recognize Odysseus when she cleans his feet? _____

   _____

Great Greek Food

While the suitors stayed at the home of Odysseus, they consumed all of his resources, including his food. They were not only unrepentant for their actions, they blamed their actions on Penelope because she wouldn't choose one of them for a husband. The Greeks had to not only prepare their own food, they had to grow it as well. Their main resources were olive trees and grapevines. Below are two recipes that you may want to prepare in class.

Tzaziki

Ingredients:

- one quart (.9 L) of Greek yogurt (or any "plain" yogurt)
- three garlic cloves
- one cucumber
- one cup (240 mL) of olive oil
- olives
- French bread or flat bread

Place the yogurt in a bowl. Place the garlic in a garlic press, and using the edge of a knife, spread the liquefied garlic lightly over the top of the yogurt. Peel the skin from the cucumber, and then cut the cucumber into very thin slices. Blend the yogurt, garlic, and cucumber slices together with a mixer while slowly drizzling the olive oil into the mixture. The oil will blend with the other ingredients. Place the mixture on a plate, and serve with a spoon and a few olives sliced over the top. Tzaziki is eaten with either a flat bread or a loaf of French bread.

Horiatiki

Ingredients:

- four tomatoes, sliced in segments
- one purple onion, sliced
- one cucumber, sliced
- feta cheese (milky, firm cheese made from goat milk), cut into cubes
- olive oil
- salt, pepper, and oregano
- flat bread

Combine tomatoes, onion, cucumber, and feta cheese together in a large bowl. Drizzle olive oil over the top. Add salt, pepper, and oregano to taste; toss lightly. Serve with a flat (unleavened) bread.

Map the Journey

The Lands Revisited

In this project, you will work with a partner to trace the journey of Odysseus. Use the map on the next page to follow the journey that Homer has described for Odysseus. You may use landmarks that are mentioned in the book, place names, and descriptions of locations. This project will involve a great deal of research, as many of these places no longer exist, or may have never existed. Begin at the island of Troy, and work out the journey to the best of your ability. Ancient maps can be downloaded from the Internet, and you can use these to trace his journey. Do your best, use the knowledge that you have gained from reading this poem, and have fun with this project!

You may wish to look at any of the Web sites listed below for additional information on mapping your journey.

Maps of Ancient Greece http://library.thinkquest.org/18650/data/lostlands/maps.html

Political Maps of Ancient Greece http://www.geocities.com/Athens/Academy/9040/maps.html

Ancient Greece Geography http://www.ancient-greece.com/geography/geography.htm

Index of Maps of Ancient Greek World http://phd.evansville.edu/tools/mapindex.htm

Historical Maps Online http://www.ukans.edu/cwis/units/kulib/maps/test.html

Interactive Ancient Mediterranean http://iam.classics.unc.edu/index.html

Journey of Odysseus http://mockingbird.creighton.edu/english/fajardo/teaching/eng120/odyjour.htm

The Journey of Odysseus http://www.oudeis.org/journey.html

Odysseus's Journey http://www.geocities.com/Athens/8497/journey.html

Map the Journey *(cont.)*

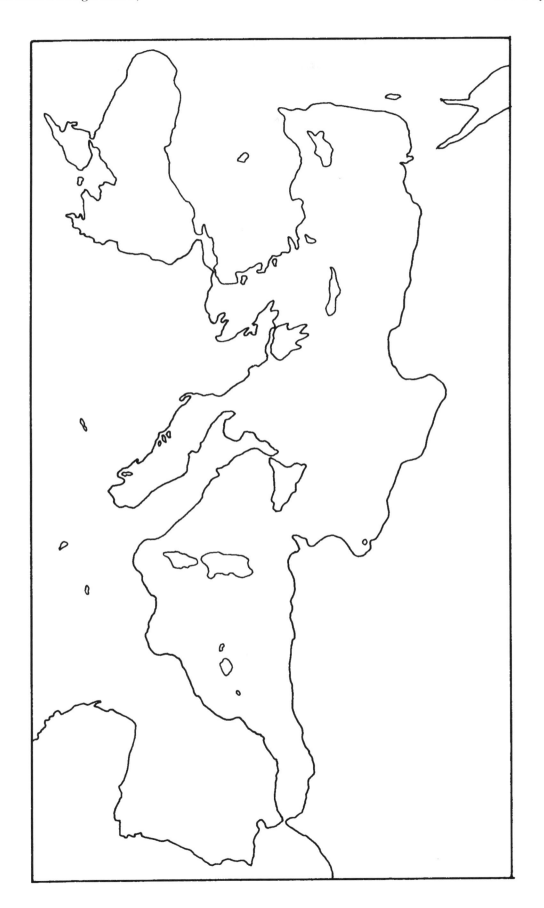

Create a Travel Brochure

Odysseus has had many adventures and traveled to numerous places during his journey. See if you can design a travel package detailing his journey. Remember to include the visits to the beautiful islands of the Phaeacians; Circes; Polyphemos; and the beautiful nymph, Calypso. Perhaps the more adventurous would like to climb the cliffs of Scylla or escape the whirlpool, Charybdis. You are limited only by your imagination. Remember to include travel details such as the best times to travel, the best times to see certain sites, and the cost involved in such a vacation!

Directions: Fold an 8½" x 11" piece of paper into thirds. When completed, you will have six sections.

Page 1: This is the cover page. Create an eye catching design that lists the name of the journey that you have decided upon. This page should also include the name of your travel company.

Page 2: This page should give a two- or three-paragraph overview of your tour. Why should people take your tour instead of one that another company offers? What are the highlights of your tour?

Page 3–4: This is the section that will give an itinerary of your tour. Be very detailed, including the various stops that you will make along the way, and the places in which you will stay overnight. Include the highlights of your tour, and the food that you will include. Make sure you include something special that only your company offers. This section should be listed by days.

Page 5: This page should list your prices. You may include peak vs. non-peak prices. For instance, if you travel to the desert in the winter, it is much more expensive than if you travel in the summer. Therefore, peak months for desert travel would be October-March, and non-peak months would be April-September. Research what the climate is like while on your tour, and determine the best times of travel. You should also decide whether your prices include taxes, food, and lodging. Make sure this is listed on your brochure.

Page 6: This will become the back page and should have a nice design, as well as the name, address, and phone number of your company.

What Would You Do?

When Odysseus returns home, he assumes the disguise of a beggar. He has been away for nearly 20 years, and there are many things that have changed in his home. He chooses wisely to take his time and examine the situation before he reveals his identity. Would you feel the same way? Select one of the following choices, and write a short essay on how you would have handled the situation.

When would you have chosen to reveal your identity? How would you have revealed it?

1. I would have disguised myself like Odysseus did, and I would reveal myself at this point:

   _____

   _____

2. I would not have disguised myself because: _____

   _____

A person shows up at your door claiming to be an old relative who you haven't seen for 20 years. Answer the following questions:

1. What would you expect as proof that the person is indeed a relative?

   _____

   _____

2. How would you expect the person to behave while he/she were visiting? (For example, would the person buy his/her own food, or maybe stay at a hotel?)

   _____

   _____

You have been away from home for many years. When you finally arrive home, how would you expect your family to treat you? Choose one of the answers below and describe your homecoming.

1. They would rejoice at my arrival and things would resume in the same manner that I left them.

   _____

   _____

2. They would treat me differently, as we would all have made many changes in our lifestyles.

   _____

   _____

What Do You Know?

1. Name two people who are cruel to Odysseus, the beggar. _____
   _____

2. Who proves himself to be a good and faithful servant? _____

3. Describe Penelope's final challenge to the suitors: _____
   _____
   _____

4. Whom does Odysseus trust to help him defeat the suitors? _____
   _____

5. Who comes the closest to stringing the bow of Odysseus? _____
   _____

6. How does Odysseus prove his true identity? _____
   _____

7. Whom does Odysseus kill first and why? _____
   _____

8. What does Odysseus do to identify and then punish the unfaithful maids? _____
   _____
   _____
   _____
   _____

9. What is done to Melanthios? _____
   _____

10. How does Penelope test Odysseus? _____
    _____

11. Why does she test him? _____
    _____

12. Who comes to battle Odysseus? _____
    _____

13. Who stops the final battle? _____

14. How does this long epic story finally end? _____
    _____
    _____

Suggested Research Topics

Students can create a 4- to 5-page research project using any of the following topics. The research paper should follow the format listed below:

Length: 4–5 pages

Format: Typed, double-spaced on 8½" x 11" (22 cm x 28 cm) sheet of paper. All essays should include a cover page and bibliography (with at least 10 sources listed).

You should submit your final work in the following order: cover page, essay, bibliography

A research paper is simple to write if you follow this simple formula: Tell why you are writing this, who it affects, how it affects them, when it was (or is) an issue, and where the reader can go for additional information.

Page 1 (Introduction): This should establish your "why" and "who" topic and serve to catch your readers attention. Give a solid reason why someone should read your paper (or why you are writing it), who it affects, and then make it interesting enough that someone would want to continue reading. Make sure that you present your thesis (topic) in a strong thesis statement at the beginning of your paper.

Pages 2–4 (Body): This section should detail the history of the topic that you are presenting and how it affects us at this point in time. You should always make sure that your thesis is strongly restated throughout your essay. Present reliable sources for any information you give on your topic.

Page 5 (Conclusion): This is the place where you restate your thesis, summarize your essay, and offer a final word on the subject.

Suggested Research Topics:

- The ritual of sacrificing animals to the Gods
- The treatment of strangers visiting in each other's homes and how they have changed
- The differences in speech between characters of different class, sex, or rank
- The use of free will in the story, and how it affects each character's life
- Death and burial rituals and belief systems (life after death, etc.) in ancient Greece
- The attributes of an epic hero
- The daily life of Ancient Greeks
- The differences and similarities in religion then and now
- A character analysis on any of the major characters
- A geographical analysis of Odysseus' journey
- A comparison of art then and art now (for example, *Star Wars* vs. *The Odyssey*)
- A comparison of the movie *The Odyssey* with the actual poem
- The use of ships in ancient times
- Different types of ships that were used during Greek times

Culminating Activities

Creating a Greek Festival

Sponsoring a Greek festival for the school can be a fantastic way of bringing the entire school together, and it can all begin in your classroom. Assign students to four groups, and distribute to each a category of the fair. Each group is responsible for selecting and organizing its activities. Each group should also have a team leader who is responsible for meeting with the leaders in other groups to schedule each activity for the day.

You should have one group in charge of organizing each of the following categories:

Activities/Games: Recruit the help of the P.E. department to organize a recreation of The Olympics, including archery (if available), cross country running, track events, etc.

Food/Drinks: Recruit the Home Economics department to help create a list of food that is Greek in origin. You can use the recipes on page 35 as a starting point. Ask the lunch personnel to assist in preparing these lunches during the day.

Decorations: Recruit the history and geography departments to help research ideas on decorating for your fair. Remember that only certain items were available for decorations (according to location), such as olive branches and grapes, and togas for costumes.

Entertainment: Ask the drama and music departments to perform songs and plays that are Greek in origin at your festival.

Each group should prepare a list of anticipated events and a completed schedule that has been approved by all group leaders. Final approval will be up to the principal and fellow teachers. For example, a completed list of events may look like this:

   **Union Middle School**

Greek Festival

Welcome to the annual Greek festival, proudly sponsored by the English Class of _____. We welcome you to participate in each of the following events!

8:00 am–9:00 am   The Greek Olympics will be held on the football field. Events include archery from 8–8:15, and track and field events for the remainder of the hour.

9:15 am–10:00 am   The drama class of _____ unfolds their presentation of *Oedipus Rex*. The play will begin promptly at 9:15 in the school auditorium.

10:15 am–11:00 am   The school band will be performing in the cafeteria as we enjoy our Greek luncheon prepared by the wonderful Home Economics department.

Noon: Come and participate in the Greek Games. Try your luck at archery or discus throwing! Awards ceremony to follow promptly at 1:00 P.M.

Unit Test Option #1

Part I Matching: Match the character's name to the description. Write the letter on the line next to the corresponding number.

_____ 1. Helen   A. wife of Odysseus

_____ 2. Laertes   B. Greek supreme god of gods

_____ 3. Mentor   C. wife of Menelaus; cause of Trojan War

_____ 4. Telemachus   D. kept Odysseus captive for nine years

_____ 5. Odysseus   E. Greek god of the seas

_____ 6. Penelope   F. one-eyed giant

_____ 7. Argos   G. father of Odysseus

_____ 8. Aeolus   H. king of Ithaca

_____ 9. Polyphemus   I. daughter of Zeus; friend of Odysseus

_____ 10. Poseidon   J. keeper of the winds

_____ 11. Zeus   K. faithful friend of Odysseus

_____ 12. Calypso   L. transforms Odysseus' crew into swine

_____ 13. Athena   M. son of Odysseus

_____ 14. Circe   N. Odysseus' hunting dog

Part II True or False Questions: To tell whether an event happened during *The Odyssey*, circle **T** for true or **F** for false.

T   F   1. A picture of a dog with a fawn in its mouth is described.

T   F   2. Zeus brings a dark cloud to rest above the ship making the men blind.

T   F   3 A bard tells the story of a fight between Odysseus and Achilles.

T   F   4. Odysseus can't swim to shore because wave swells will smash him against the rocks.

T   F   5. Odysseus has a sweet drink, a drink for the gods.

T   F   6. Odysseus discovers crates heaped with cheese and pens crowded with lambs.

T   F   7. Four black stallions pull Odysseus' ship off of the sandbar.

T   F   8. Odysseus brings back his men by force and binds them.

Unit Test Option #2

Short Essay: Answer each of the following questions using specific details from the text.

1. Explain how Penelope tests Odysseus upon his return. _____
   _____
   _____

2. Why don't the other Cyclops giants help Polyphemus? _____
   _____
   _____

3. What is Scylla? _____
   _____
   _____

4. How does Penelope's nurse recognize Odysseus? _____
   _____
   _____

5. Who is Circe? _____
   _____
   _____

6. Explain "in media res." _____
   _____
   _____

7. Explain the importance of "Noman." _____
   _____
   _____

8. Why do you think *The Odyssey* is considered a classic when very few poems ever make it to epic status? _____
   _____
   _____

9. List two literary techniques that allowed poets to memorize such lengthy poems. _____
   _____
   _____

10. List the four main attributes of an epic, and explain how *The Odyssey* fulfills this definition. _____
    _____
    _____

Unit Test Option #3

Conversations

Work in size-appropriate groups to write and perform the conversation that might have occurred in one of the following situations.

- Penelope and her son, Telemachus, discuss his father's absence and how they will cope during this time. *(2 persons)*

- Penelope asks the suitors to leave her palace. *(3–6 persons)*

- Telemachus speaks with Athena on the location of his father, but she is ordered by Zeus not to disclose this information. *(3 persons)*

- Penelope and Odysseus discuss their expectations for Telemachus' life prior to Odysseus leaving home. *(2 persons)*

- Imagine that Odysseus finds his son, Telemachus, when he enters Hades. *(2 persons)*

- Place *The Odyssey* in today's time, and discuss how Odysseus reacts when he comes home and finds the suitors at his home. How would he handle the situation in this day and age? *(5–6 persons)*

- Discuss the life of Telemachus if he had chosen to stay in Ithaca rather than search for his father. *(3–6 persons)*

- Imagine that Odysseus was alone when he encountered the Cyclops. How would he have handled the situation at that point? How could he have discussed other options with the Cyclops? *(2 persons)*

- Recreate a conversation with a person whom Odysseus meets in Hades. This could be his mother, Thesius, or any of his crew members. *(2 persons)*

- Create a discussion between Odysseus and some of the leaders who recruited him to go to war in Troy. How do they convince him to leave his family? *(3–4 persons)*

- Telemachus approaches the suitors and requests they leave his home. *(3–6 persons)*

- Imagine that one of the suitors recognizes Odysseus upon his return to the island. How does he handle this new-found knowledge? *(2–4 persons)*

Bibliography and Resources

Books

Bassett, S.E. *The Poetry of Homer*. Berkeley: University of California Press, 1938.

Evslin, Bernard, Dorothy Evslin, and Ned Hoopes. *The Greek Gods.* New York: Scholastic, Inc., 1966.

Evslin, Bernard, Dorothy Evslin, and Ned Hoopes. *Heroes & Monsters of Greek Myths*. New York: Scholastic, Inc., 1966.

Fagles, Robert. *The Odyssey*. New York: Penguin Books, 1996.

Fleischman, Paul. *Dateline: Troy. Cambridg*e: Candlewick Press, 1996.

Graves, Robert. *The Greek Myths*. Baltimore: Penguin Books, 1955.

Mandelbaum, Allen. *The Odyssey of Homer.* New York: Bantam Books, 1991.

Milch, Robert J. and Brooklyn Colleges. *Homer's, The Odyssey* (Cliff's Notes). Lincoln, NE: Cliff's Notes Inc., 1996.

Reek, Michael. *Homer's Iliad*. New York: Icon Editions, 1994.

Web Sites

Ancient Greece Geography—http://www.ancient-greece.com/geography/geography.htm

Greek Mythology: Odysseus—http://www.mythweb.com/odyssey

Historical Maps Menu—http://www.ukans.edu/cwis/units/kulib/maps/test.html

Index of Maps of Ancient Greek World—http://phd.evansville.edu/tools/mapindex.htm

Interactive Ancient Mediterranean—http://iam.classics.unc.edu/index.html

Internet Classics Archive—http://classics.mit.edu/Homer/odyssey.html

Journey of Odysseus—http://mockingbird.creighton.edu/english/fajardo/teaching/eng120/odyjour.htm

The Journey of Odysseus—http://www.oudeis.org/journey.html

Maps of Ancient Greece—http://library.thinkquest.org/18650/data/lostlands/maps.html

Odysseus's Journey—http://www.geocities.com/Athens/8497/journey.html

Greek Mythology: Odysseus—http://www.mythweb.com/odyssey

Political Maps of Ancient Greece—http://www.geocities.com/Athens/Academy/9040/maps.html

Answer Key

Page 18
1. T
2. T
3. F
4. T
5. F
6. F
7. T
8. T
9. F
10. F
11. T
12. T

Page 23
1. the Muses
2. 20 years
3. Mentes
4. two eagles
5. Penelope
6. unweaving the shroud that she weaves all day
7. hold an assembly, then sail into the world
8. ambush and kill him
9. Poseidon
10. Menelaous
11. Athena
12. immortality
13. Pylos
14. nine bulls
15. a great feast to celebrate upcoming weddings of the King's son and daughter
16. Hermes
17. the island of Ogygia
18. the island of Scheria, the home of the Phaeacians
19. Princess Nausicaa
20. Athena appears to her in a dream

Page 24
1. XV
2. DCCLIX
3. MM
4. MXXIX
5. CCLXXX
6. CDXCIII
7. MML

8. CMXXVIII
9. XLVIII
10. CCCXC
11. CCXXIV
12. DCCIL

Page 29
1. They did not want to return home.
2. He anticipates trouble with the Cyclops.
3. Polyphemos
4. Poseidon
5. god of the winds
6. Island of the Laestrygonians
7. Ogygia
8. swine
9. Tiresius, the prophet
10. nymphs who sing a hypnotic song which draws men to them
11. Odysseus ties himself to the mast of the boat and forces his men to plug their ears with wax.
12. a whirlpool
13. a six-headed monster
14. never to raise the sun again
15. He learned from the Phaeicians.
16. Athena
17. reveals himself to his son
18. with caution

Page 34
1. by the magic ship of the Phaeicians
2. Athena
3. as an old man
4. They are struck by a large tidal wave.
5. Telemachus
6. The dog sees him, draws a breath, and dies.
7. Antinous
8. Irus considers Ithaca his personal begging ground, and will not tolerate competition.
9. This is what the state that Odysseus loves has been reduced to in his absence, but now that he has returned, all will become as it should be.
10. A scar

Answer Key *(cont.)*

Page 40

1. Antinous, Irus
2. Eumaeus
3. string the bow of Odysseus, and shoot an arrow cleanly through a straight row of 12 axes
4. Telemachus
5. Telemachus
6. by being upset about the destruction of his and Penelope's bed
7. Antinous, because he was the leader
8. He asks Eurycleia to identify them, then brings them into the hall and forces them to clean the floors after moving the corpses away. He then takes them out and has them hanged.
9. He is executed and mutilated.
10. She speaks of the destruction of their wedding bed.
11. because she is intelligent and cunning, just like Odysseus
12. the angry kinsmen of the slain suitors
13. Athena
14. Answers may vary.

Pages 43

Part I: Matching

1. C
2. G
3. K
4. M
5. H
6. A
7. N
8. J
9. F
10. E
11. B
12. D
13. I
14. L

Part II: True-False Questions.

1. T
2. F
3 F
4. T
5. T

6. T
7. F
8. T

Page 44

1. She tells him that their bed has been torn down.
2. because he shouts that "No man" poked out his eye, and they don't believe he is serious.
3. a huge six-headed monster that lives on a cliff and devours passing sailors
4. by a scar on his leg
5. a witch who lives on an island and turns Odysseus' men into swine
6. beginning in the middle of things
7. This is what Odysseus told Polyphemos his name was so that when he yelled for help, nobody would come to his aid.
8. This is a poem, and very few people endeavor to recreate a poem of this length by following the standards such work requires.
9. epithets, similes, or formal rhetoric
10. It contains adventure, it has a central heroic figure, the setting is vast—often covering the entire world, supernatural forces are involved, and an elevated style is used. (Examples may vary.)

Page 45

Accept appropriate answers.